ROSEN Verified
THE BILL OF RIGHTS

What Is Unreasonable Search and Seizure?

Kathleen A. Klatte

ROSEN
PUBLISHING

Published in 2024 by The Rosen Publishing Group, Inc.
2544 Clinton Street, Buffalo, NY 14224

First Edition

Editor: Greg Roza
Book Design: Michael Flynn

Photo Credits: Cover LightField Studios; (series background) PinkPueblo/Shutterstock.com; p. 5 zimmytws/Shutterstock.com; p. 6 courtesy of the Library of Congress; https://commons.wikimedia.org/wiki/File:Thompson-Advance.jpg; p. 8 https://commons.wikimedia.org/wiki/File:J._(James)_Otis_(NYPL_Hades-251018-465420).jpg; p. 9 Voinakh/Shutterstock.com; p. 11 (main) Cris Kelly/Shutterstock.com; p. 13 chippix/Shutterstock.com; p. 11 (inset) ponsulak /Shutterstock.com; p. 15 Leonard Zhukovsky/Shutterstock.com; p. 17 Michael O'Keene/Shutterstock.com; p. 19 CLP Media/Shutterstock.com; p. 20 Brian A Jackson/Shutterstock.com; p. 21 Rawpixel.com/Shutterstock.com; p. 23 sdecoret/Shutterstock.com; p. 25 PeopleImages.com - Yuri A/Shutterstock.com; p. 27 Carolina K. Smith MD/Shutterstock.com; p. 29 courtesy of U.S. Immigration and Customs Enforcement; p. 30 artboySHF/Shutterstock.com; p. 31 https://commons.wikimedia.org/wiki/File:Supreme_Court_of_the_United_States_-_Roberts_Court_2022.jpg; p. 33 Si Vo/Shutterstock.com; p. 35 https://commons.wikimedia.org/wiki/File:CBP_Border_Patrol_agent_reads_the_Miranda_rights.jpg; p. 37 Tupungato/Shutterstock.com; p. 39 Everett Collection/Shutterstock.com; p. 41 Microgen/Shutterstock.com; p. 42 Andrey_Popov/Shutterstock.com; p. 43 aslysun/Shutterstock.com; p. 45 javierIvarezm/Shutterstock.com.

Cataloging-in-Publication Data

Names: Klatte, Kathleen A.
Title: What is unreasonable search and seizure? / Kathleen A. Klatte.
Description: New York : Rosen Publishing, 2024. | Series: Rosen verified: the Bill of Rights | Includes glossary and index.
Identifiers: ISBN 9781499469691 (pbk.) | ISBN 9781499469707 (library bound) | ISBN 9781499469714 (ebook)
Subjects: LCSH: Searches and seizures--United States--Juvenile literature.
Classification: LCC KF9630.K53 2024 | DDC 345.73'0722--dc23

Manufactured in the United States of America

Some of the images in this book illustrate individuals who are models. The depictions do not imply actual situations or events.

CPSIA Compliance Information: Batch #CSRYA24. For further information contact Rosen Publishing at 1-800-237-9932.

Find us on

CONTENTS

The Fourth Amendment

The first 10 amendments to the constitution of the United States are called the Bill of Rights. These are very special rights. The Founding Fathers thought they were so important that they needed to be listed and given special **protection**.

The Fourth Amendment **guarantees** protection from unreasonable search and seizure. But what does that mean? And who gets this protection?

These are questions Americans have been asking for more than 200 years. Many of the things we think of as private—such as phones, photographs, and cars—didn't exist when the Bill of Rights was written. The meaning of citizenship has changed over time too. So just what does the Fourth Amendment mean to us today?

THE TEXT OF AMENDMENT IV

"The right of the people to be secure in their persons, houses, papers, and effects, against unreasonable searches and seizures, shall not be violated, and no **warrants** shall issue, but upon probable cause, supported by oath or affirmation, and particularly describing the place to be searched, and the persons or things to be seized."

The Bill of Rights

When the U.S. Constitution was written, people wanted to be sure that the new government would have limits. They wanted a list of rights that would always be protected. That list became the first 10 amendments to the Constitution. It's called the Bill of Rights.

A Bill of Rights

as provided in the Ten Original Amendments to

The Constitution of the United States

in force December 15, 1791.

Article I

Congress shall make no law respecting an establishment of religion, or prohibiting the free exercise thereof; or abridging the freedom of speech, or of the press; or the right of the people peaceably to assemble, and to petition the Government for a redress of grievances.

Article II

A well regulated Militia, being necessary to the security of a free State, the right of the people to keep and bear Arms, shall not be infringed.

Article III

No Soldier shall, in time of peace be quartered in any house, without the consent of the Owner, nor in time of war, but in a manner to be prescribed by law.

Article IV

The right of the people to be secure in their persons, houses, papers, and effects, against unreasonable searches and seizures, shall not be violated, and no Warrants shall issue, but upon probable cause, supported by Oath or affirmation, and particularly describing the place to be searched, and the persons or things to be seized.

Article V

No person shall be held to answer for a capital, or otherwise infamous crime, unless on a presentment or indictment of a Grand Jury, except in cases arising in the land or naval forces, or in the Militia, when in actual service in time of War or public danger; nor shall any person be subject for the same offence to be twice put in jeopardy of life or limb; nor shall be compelled in any Criminal Case to be a witness against himself, nor be deprived of life, liberty, or property, without due process of law; nor shall private property be taken for public use, without just compensation.

Article VI

In all criminal prosecutions, the accused shall enjoy the right to a speedy and public trial, by an impartial jury of the State and district wherein the crime shall have been committed, which district shall have been previously ascertained by law, and to be informed of the nature and cause of the accusation; to be confronted with the witnesses against him; to have compulsory process for obtaining Witnesses in his favor, and to have the Assistance of Counsel for his defence.

Article VII

In Suits at common law, where the value in controversy shall exceed twenty dollars, the right of trial by jury shall be preserved, and no fact tried by a jury shall be otherwise re-examined in any Court of the United States, than according to the rules of the common law.

Article VIII

Excessive bail shall not be required, nor excessive fines imposed, nor cruel and unusual punishments inflicted.

Article IX

The enumeration in the Constitution, of certain rights, shall not be construed to deny or disparage others retained by the people.

Article X

The powers not delegated to the United States by the Constitution, nor prohibited by it to the States, are reserved to the States respectively, or to the people.

*Regards of
Harry B. Nairs.*

People created these amendments because of things the British government did to the colonies. Some of them don't seem as important now. Special judges called Supreme Court justices decide how the amendments apply today.

Prior to and during the American Revolution, British soldiers often entered private homes. They would arrest people or take things. The Bill of Rights prevents that sort of thing from happening today.

What Did It Mean Then?

In colonial times, the British used papers called "writs of assistance" as well as other similar papers. These allowed soldiers to go anywhere they wanted. They could search anything and take whatever they wanted. They didn't need a clear **legal** reason for what they did.

JAMES OTIS

James Otis was a lawyer, or someone whose job is to help people with the law. He worked for the British government. He quit his job because he thought the law was unfair to colonists. He was elected to the Massachusetts legislature, or law-making body. He worked with Samuel Adams and others.

The Founding Fathers wrote the Fourth Amendment to make sure this didn't happen in the new country. The Fourth Amendment says that a place can't be searched without a warrant. A warrant is written by a judge. Police can only use it to search a **specific** place.

The Founding Fathers didn't think colonists were treated fairly. They thought that British law should protect all citizens, not just those in Great Britain.

What Does It Mean Now?

The Fourth Amendment mentions things like houses and papers because that's what was familiar to people at the time. Today we also store **information** on computers and smartphones. We travel in cars. We record things **digitally** and take photos.

Laws have changed over time to account for all these things. Judges decide how the law applies to new **technology**. Sometimes there are disagreements about what's legal. These arguments are sometimes settled by the Supreme Court.

FROM PHONE BOOTHS TO SMARTPHONES

Katz v. United States of 1967 was a U.S. Supreme Court case about the privacy of public phone booths. This technology was something the Founding Fathers never imagined. It's now totally out of date! However, the idea that phone calls are private, no matter where they're made, still stands.

In the case *Riley v. California* (2014), the Supreme Court ruled that police officers may seize a cell phone from a person who is under arrest, but may not search the cell phone without a warrant.

Reasonable vs. Unreasonable

Modern police forces exist to prevent and solve, or figure out, crimes. To solve crimes, they need to collect **evidence**. The Fourth Amendment exists to make sure that police act in a way that's fair.

Our legal system is based on the idea that a person is innocent, or didn't do anything wrong, until proven **guilty**. This means basing a case on facts. It also means following all the rules. These steps are meant to make sure that innocent people aren't searched or arrested unlawfully.

UNREASONABLE	REASONABLE
Questioning a person of color who happens to be near a crime scene.	Questioning someone who looks a lot like the person the victim **described**.
Searching a house without a warrant.	Searching a house after getting a warrant based on evidence.
Pulling over a car because the driver looks different.	Pulling over a car because it's zigzagging all over the road.

The first modern police force was formed in Boston in 1838.
Before that, soldiers or night watchmen kept the peace.

What's Probable Cause?

Probable cause is evidence that someone might be guilty of a crime. Police aren't supposed to arrest a person without a good reason. The reason must be clear and based on facts. This could be a description of a person or the license plate number of a car.

Police can't just search anyplace they want. They need probable cause to ask a judge for a search warrant. They also need probable cause to pull over a car or question someone.

Police can pull over a car if the driver is breaking a traffic law. They can also stop a car if they **suspect** that the driver is drunk based on how that person is driving.

Racial Profiling

The term "racial profiling" refers to situations in which a person is thought to be guilty of a crime just because of the color of their skin. It's illegal to target, or suspect, someone just because of their race. An **investigation** needs to be based on facts.

Police shouldn't investigate a person unless there is evidence. A case shouldn't be based on race unless there's film or an **eyewitness** account.

AN ONGOING PROBLEM

Racism has been a problem in the United States for a long time. This has led to cases of racial profiling. Some police might also not fully investigate crimes committed against African Americans or other people of color.

Police can look specifically for someone who fits a description given by people who saw a crime committed. That description may include skin color.

What's a Search Warrant?

A search warrant is a paper written and signed by a judge. This sort of warrant gives permission to search private property. To get one, police must explain why they think they'll find evidence of a crime in a certain place. They must also explain what they hope to find, such as a gun.

Police can only search the place named in the warrant. They can only look where they can reasonably expect to find what they're searching for. (They can't open a small container to look for something big.)

Even with a warrant, police aren't supposed to just break into a place. They must knock, announce themselves, and provide the warrant.

Privacy in the Digital Age

As people create new technology, judges have to change the way they **interpret** the law. What tends to happen is that police seize evidence that's in a new form. A lawyer questions if it was legal to collect that evidence. This might result in another court case. Some cases go all the way to the Supreme Court. There have been court cases about cars, phone records, and emails.

There are many court cases about the privacy of **data**. Your own computer is probably considered private. One that belongs to your school or job might not be.

United States v. Microsoft Corp.

In 2013, the company Microsoft was served with a warrant. It was asked to provide a client's data. Microsoft refused to turn over data that was on a server in Ireland. It said the warrant didn't apply to data stored in another country.

Fourth Amendment **scholars** agreed that the original warrant didn't apply to data stored in another country. (Remember, warrants must be very specific!) As time passed, the law changed so the case didn't apply anymore.

FRIEND OF THE COURT

Amicus curiae is Latin for "friend of the court." In *United States v. Microsoft Corp.*, this referred to experts on the Fourth Amendment. They explained why the amendment should apply in this case.

One of the laws referred to in the Microsoft case is the Stored Communications Act (SCA). The law has since been changed. It now says warrants can be issued for data stored overseas. Some people question if this is legal.

Carpenter v. United States

Carpenter v. United States from 2018 was a case about cell phone records. The FBI used evidence from cell phone records to arrest Timothy Carpenter. They didn't have a search warrant to look at these records. Carpenter's lawyers said this went against his Fourth Amendment rights.

The Supreme Court ruled in Carpenter's favor. Five justices agreed it was an unreasonable search and seizure. They said that people had the right to expect their phone calls to be private.

PRIVATE!

Many court cases use the phrase "reasonable expectation of privacy." Generally, this means that things that have to be opened or unlocked are private. You need a key to get into your home. This means your home should be private.

Our society usually considers conversations, or talks between people, to be private. This idea covers telephone conversations. The court has decided that police need warrants, even for pay phones and cell phones.

The Needs of the Many

Sometimes, public good is considered more important than personal privacy. The Patriot Act is a law that was passed after the 9/11 terrorist attacks. This law permitted police to collect cell phone and internet records without a warrant.

Many people felt that it was a serious **invasion of privacy**. They said it was a violation of, or attack on, constitutional rights. Others argued that it was worth it to protect the public from another attack. What do you think?

Airport security, or guards, can search people and their luggage. They don't need warrants or probable cause.

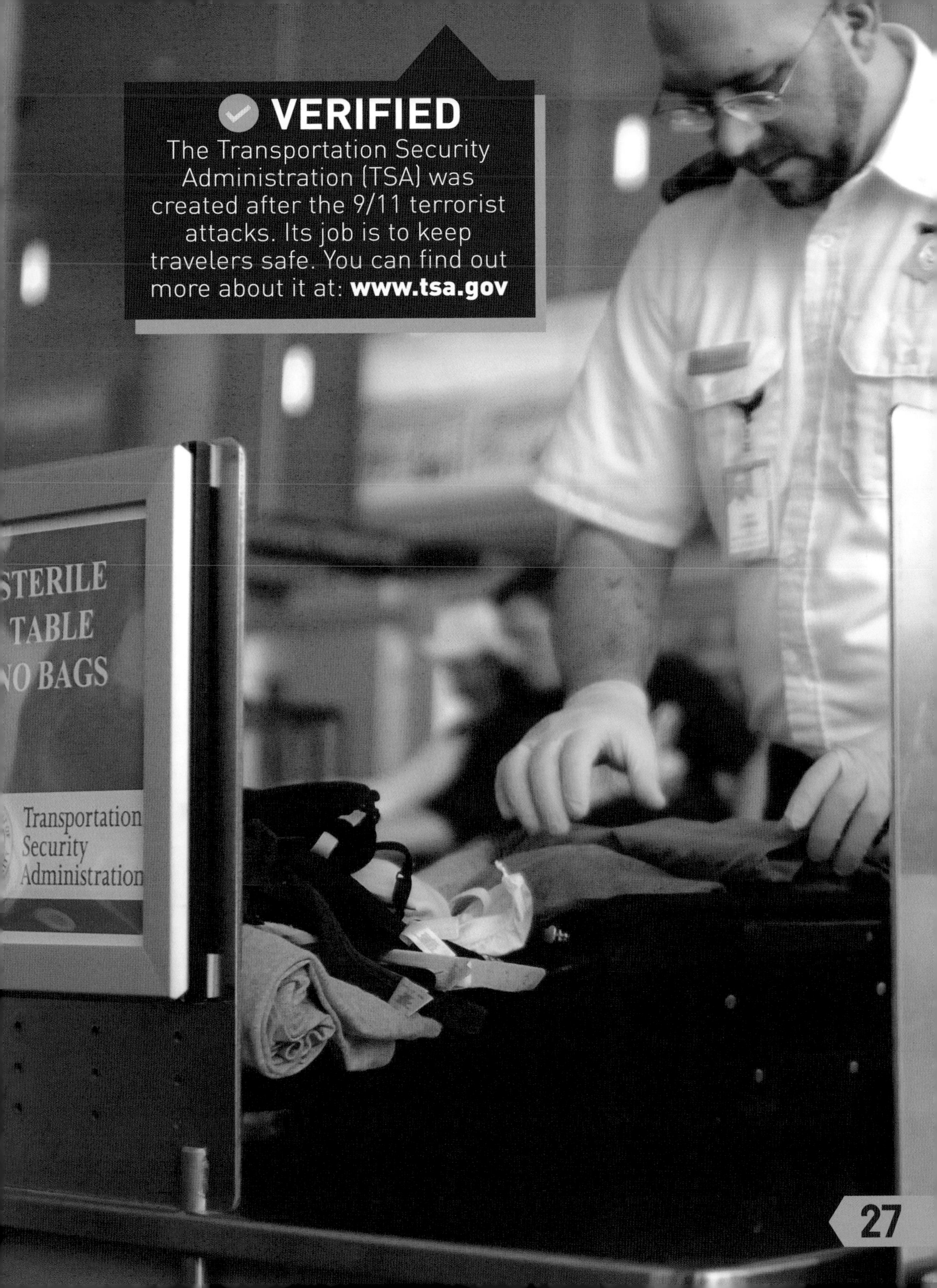

STERILE
TABLE
NO BAGS

Transportation
Security
Administration

Who's Protected?

Just whose rights are protected by the Constitution? According to the 14th Amendment, it protects everyone living in the United States. The 14th Amendment was adopted in 1868. It was written to protect the rights of people who had been enslaved.

The 14th Amendment doesn't just apply to citizens. It says that any person is entitled to equal protection of the law. This means immigrants, or noncitizens who've come to live in the United States. This is why some people have questioned the actions of U.S. border patrols in recent years.

HOT TOPIC

For hundreds of years, people have come to America to have a better life. Many immigrants have gone on to do a lot for society. However, some Americans feel too many immigrants are coming to the United States. U.S. Immigration and Customs Enforcement (ICE) is a federal agency that enforces U.S. immigration laws. This is a tough job. It's nearly impossible to stop all illegal immigration.

In 2022, 2.8 million immigrants were arrested or turned away from the U.S. border.

✅ VERIFIED

Many people today question ICE's actions. It has separated families trying to enter the United States. It often holds children in different camps from their parents. The camps may have no doctors or teachers. What do you think? You can find out more about ICE at its website: **www.ice.gov**

Who Decides What's Private?

The Fourth Amendment says that police need a warrant to enter a house. They don't always need a warrant to search a car. But what about a mobile home? Is that a house or a vehicle?

Sometimes the Supreme Court changes old decisions. This might be because of new technology. It can also be because of changes in our society.

What do you think would surprise the Founding Fathers more—
the cases heard today, or the judges who decide them?

These are the sort of questions that the Supreme Court often decides. The Supreme Court is the most important court in the United States. Its job is to decide how the Constitution applies to current society.

What About School?

Do students have a right to privacy at school? That's a hard question. Kids do have rights. But school leaders are responsible for all the kids in a school. It's their job to make sure that the school is a safe and orderly place for kids to learn.

School officials usually don't need a warrant from a judge to search a student. They must have "reasonable **suspicion**" that a law or school rule was broken. This isn't the same as probable cause.

NEW JERSEY V. T.L.O.

New Jersey v. T.L.O. was a case about a student whose purse was searched by a school official. The official didn't have a search warrant. The court ruled that the need for everyone to be safe at school is more important than one person's privacy.

Lockers and desks are school property. Generally, school officials can search them. However, they can't search a student's property without reasonable suspicion.

The Exclusionary Rule

Most questions about the Fourth Amendment have to do with the way evidence is gathered for a case. The police have a job to do. The purpose of the Fourth Amendment is to be sure that they follow all the rules.

When police seize evidence without a warrant, that evidence can be dismissed. This is called the "exclusionary rule." It exists to protect people from abuses, or misuses, of power that were common in the colonial era.

MIRANDA RIGHTS

"You have the right to remain silent. Anything you say can and will be used against you in a court of law. You have the right to speak to a lawyer, and to have a lawyer present during any questioning. If you cannot afford a lawyer, one will be provided for you at government expense."

Miranda v. Arizona was a case from 1966. It says that if police take statements from a suspect without first reading their rights, the statements can be thrown out of court. This is like the exclusionary rule.

Other Important Cases

Police can't search your home without a warrant. But what about your car? This question came up in the early 20th century. Judges decided that police usually don't need a warrant to search a car if they have probable cause. This is because a car can easily be moved.

Are phone calls private? In 1967, the court ruled that calls made from pay phones were considered private. We don't really use pay phones anymore. So, what about cell phones? Your own cell phone is private—one that belongs to your workplace isn't.

California v. Carney was a case from 1985. It says that police don't need a warrant to search a motor home. This is because a motor home is also a vehicle that can be easily moved. They do need to have probable cause.

KEY CASES

1925	*Carroll v. U.S.*	Police usually don't need a warrant to search a car.
1967	*Katz v. U.S.*	Police need a warrant to record telephone calls.
1968	*Terry v. Ohio*	Evidence obtained without a warrant can't be used.
2001	*Kyllo v. U.S.*	Use of thermal, or heat, imaging requires a warrant.
2010	*Ontario v. Quon*	Equipment that belongs to a workplace isn't considered private.

The ACLU

The American Civil Liberties Union (ACLU) is a civil rights group. It was founded in 1920 to make sure that everyone is protected by the Bill of Rights. It does this by working within the legal system.

ACLU lawyers represent people in court cases. They also write reports about the meaning of the law. They are often involved, or take part, in cases about the Fourth Amendment. The ACLU has been involved in many milestone cases about privacy.

✔ VERIFIED

You can learn more about the ACLU at its website:
www.aclu.org

A. Mitchell Palmer was the U.S. attorney general right after World War I. He arrested and deported people he thought were **Communists**, or forced them to leave the country. He often had no way to prove this. This is the first cause the ACLU became involved in.

Police Technology

Modern police forces are supposed to exist to protect society. Police tend to see new technology as a good way to do this. Questions often occur when police use a new tool to gather evidence. Just because they can find out things from a distance doesn't always mean it's right. Looking at a building with **thermal imaging** is still a search. So is collecting cell phone information. Police still need to show probable cause and get a warrant.

This police scientist is looking at evidence. She's being very careful not to **contaminate** it. This is to make sure the right person is arrested.

Facial Recognition

Facial recognition is a newer technology. It matches a photo of a person to a database of photos. This allows users to find out a person's name and location. Police think this could be a good tool for solving crimes. Many other people think it's a very bad invasion of privacy.

Suppose anyone could snap a picture of you and find out all your information. That's a scary idea.

READ IT!

Most websites have terms of service (TOS). They may be printed in tiny letters and have lots of long words. Most people just click to make the box with this information go away. The TOS says how your information can be used by the website—you may want to read it before continuing!

People post pictures to social media for fun. They don't think about those pictures being collected for a database.

There are questions about where the information in databases comes from. Many people worry about this kind of personal information being misused. Some computer companies thought it was such a bad idea that they stopped working on it.

Changing with the Times

Sometimes events in the world can affect the way our laws are adapted, or changed, and applied. In 2020, a new disease called COVID-19 spread around the world. Many people around the world became very sick.

The governor of Rhode Island told police to stop cars with New York State license plates. This was because there were so many sick people in New York. Some people said this was a violation of the Fourth Amendment. The governor argued that she was trying to keep the people of her state safe. What she wanted was good, but the way she tried to do it was against the letter of the law.

This is the sort of thing that legal scholars and judges will continue to study. This is how our constitution changes with the times.

Driving a car with a New York license plate doesn't break any laws. It's not probable cause to stop a car. Legally, this is an unreasonable search and seizure.

Communist: A person who believes in Communism, a system of government in which a single party controls state-owned means of production.

contaminate: To pollute.

data: Facts and figures, information.

describe: To tell someone what something is like.

digital: Using or marked by computer technology.

evidence: Material that is presented to a court of law to help find the truth about something.

eyewitness: A person who sees something happen and can describe it.

guarantee: To promise that something will happen or be done.

guilty: Responsible for committing a crime or doing something bad or wrong.

information: Facts or details about a subject.

interpret: To explain or tell the meaning of something.

invasion of privacy: A situation in which someone tries to get information about a person's private life in an unwanted and usually improper way.

investigation: The act of trying to find out the facts about something, such as a crime or an accident.

legal: Based on the law.

protection: Something that keeps someone or something safe.

racism: The belief that some races of people are better than others.

scholar: Someone who has done advanced study in a field.

specific: Clearly and exactly presented or stated: precise or exact.

suspect: To think that (someone) is possibly guilty of a crime or of doing something wrong.

suspicion: A feeling that something is wrong without proof.

technology: A method that uses science to solve problems and the tools used to solve those problems.

thermal imaging: Using the heat given off by an object to produce an image of it or to locate it.

warrant: A document issued by a court that gives the police the power to do something.

INDEX